CLIMATE CHANGE

SOCIAL SOLUTIONS

BY JIM OLLHOFF

Visit us at
www.abdopublishing.com

Published by ABDO Publishing Company, 8000 West 78th Street, Suite 310, Edina, MN 55439. Copyright ©2011 by Abdo Consulting Group, Inc. International copyrights reserved in all countries. No part of this book may be reproduced in any form without written permission from the publisher. ABDO & Daughters™ is a trademark and logo of ABDO Publishing Company.

Printed in the United States of America, North Mankato, Minnesota
052010
092010

 PRINTED ON RECYCLED PAPER

Editor: John Hamilton
Graphic Design: Sue Hamilton
Cover Photos: Thinkstock, iStockphoto
Interior Photo: Alamy-pg 19; AP-pgs 5, 6, 7, 9, 12, 14, 15, 17, 18, 23 & 27; Corbis-pg 21; Environmental Protection Agency-pg 26; Getty Images-pgs 11, 13 & 16; iStockphoto-pgs 10, 20, 24, 25 & 28; Photo Researchers-pgs 22 & 29; Thinkstock-pgs 1 & 32.

Library of Congress Cataloging-in-Publication Data

Ollhoff, Jim.
   Social solutions / Jim Ollhoff.
      p. cm. -- (Climate change)
   Includes index.
   ISBN 978-1-61613-456-3
   1. Climatic changes--Prevention--Juvenile literature. 2. Climatic changes--Prevention--Citizen participation--Juvenile literature. 3. Global warming--Prevention--Juvenile literature. 4. Global warming--Prevention--Citizen participation--Juvenile literature. I. Title.
   QC903.15.O45 2010
   363.738'74--dc22
                  2010005510

CONTENTS

SOLUTIONS TO CLIMATE CHANGE

Solutions to climate change are easy to talk about, but hard to accomplish. The problem could be solved if people quit putting carbon dioxide and other greenhouse gasses into the atmosphere. That is easy to say, but there are many challenges that keep us from doing it.

Some people think that technology will be the solution. That might be true. Scientists might come up with a way to fix the climate. However, history shows us that technological solutions usually create new problems.

Instead of relying on technology, it might be better to find social solutions. In other words, it may be more effective to solve the problem with changes in thinking and behavior, and in agreements between world leaders.

People know that in order to stop global warming, big changes need to happen. So far, the world's leaders haven't been able to make the necessary changes. The world is at a point where small efforts will not stop climate change. To stop it, we need big transformations, sweeping agreements, and the involvement of every part of society.

Above: Instead of driving cars, many people use bicycles and public transportation to get to work.

CAN THE WORLD'S GOVERNMENTS COOPERATE?

Below: Supporters of the Kyoto Protocol dressed in bear costumes to encourage world leaders to protect the world's climate and all living things.

Climate change is a global problem. It is important that all governments work together to find solutions. The first big climate change conference was held in Kyoto, Japan, in 1997. At this meeting, world leaders created a document called the Kyoto Protocol. It was a voluntary agreement to reduce greenhouse gasses that cause global warming.

In 2001, the United States withdrew its support for the Kyoto Protocol agreement. President George W. Bush said the rules were unfair to developed nations like the United States, and would hurt the economy.

A New Dawn of Climate Protection February 16 2005 KYOTO PROTO Entry into Force

Above: President Obama at the United Nations conference in Copenhagen, Denmark, 2009.

The United Nations held another conference in December 2009, in Copenhagen, Denmark. At this meeting, leaders agreed again that greenhouse gasses must be limited. During the past 100 years, the world's average climate temperature rose about 1 degree Celsius (1.8 degrees F). The Copenhagen agreement tried to limit greenhouse gasses. It said that global temperatures should rise no more than another 2 degrees Celsius (3.6 degrees F). However, the Copenhagen agreement does not force governments to follow the rules. The limits on greenhouse gasses are only voluntary.

It will take many nations, working together, to reduce greenhouse gas emissions. They also have to deal with the consequences of a warmer world. So far, world leaders have failed to create a perfect plan to deal with climate change.

WHAT CAN NATIONAL GOVERNMENTS DO?

It is important for governments in North America to encourage the use of renewable energy, especially wind and solar energy. New wind and solar power plants would mean fewer fossil fuel power plants, and less carbon dioxide spewing into the atmosphere.

North America's electrical grid also needs to be updated. Many parts of the electrical grid are very old. A new, more efficient electrical grid is needed. Since solar power doesn't produce electricity at night, and wind power doesn't produce electricity in calm weather, the electrical grid needs to be able to handle the on-and-off nature of renewable energy.

Many countries in Europe have greatly increased the use of solar and wind power. Europeans have passed laws requiring utility companies to buy back extra electricity from homes. For example, a home might have a solar collector that generates electricity. If the house doesn't use all of the electricity that it generates, then the utility companies buy that electricity to use it elsewhere.

Facing Page:
The Dutch have used wind power for centuries. A traditional windmill and modern wind turbines stand side-by-side in Zoeterwoude, Netherlands.

Another important thing governments can do is stop desertification. Desertification happens when farmland turns into desert, or deserts expand. Poor soil management and farming techniques cause soil to become overused and depleted of nutrients. Few plants grow in the poor soil, and it becomes desert. This kind of soil holds very little carbon. National governments can make laws to encourage farmers to manage their land better and replenish the soil.

Another problem is deforestation. This happens when companies slash and burn forests to make room for something else, like cattle grazing or mining. This is a big problem in countries like Brazil and parts of Africa. Land is often cleared for agriculture. Other times, companies simply want lumber to sell, and don't bother replanting. Deforestation is a double problem for global warming. Forests that converted carbon dioxide to oxygen are now gone. And when forests are burned, massive amounts of soot enter the atmosphere. Soot traps more of the sun's heat. National governments can make laws about deforestation. They can prohibit it in some areas, or require that companies replant trees.

There are many other things governments can do. They can require new cars to be more energy efficient and travel farther on a tank of gasoline. Governments can set limits on greenhouse gasses. They can tax companies that produce too much carbon dioxide. Governments can be part of the solution to climate change. Unfortunately, political leaders are often reluctant to make laws until there is intense pressure from citizens.

Above:

Deforestation in the Amazon rainforest. Huge forests are cleared for lumber, or to make room for agriculture, livestock grazing, or mining.

Above and Left: Desertification happens when areas are cleared and farmland turns into desert. The soil may become overused and depleted of nutrients. Sandstorms are common in areas where this has happened.

WHAT CAN BUSINESSES DO?

Facing Page: In 2009, California's Big Blue Bus facility installed solar arrays and other environmentally friendly features in their new building. *Below:* Introduced in 2010, Frito-Lay's SunChips packages break down in oxygen and water.

Businesses and industries are often big polluters. Manufacturing processes can be dirty and wasteful. But some companies have led the way in creating green and carbon-free processes.

For example, some companies have invested in solar power. They have filled their roofs with photovoltaic cells, which convert sunlight directly into electricity. Other companies have put up windmills, or simply bought renewable energy from utility companies.

Some companies have reduced their wasteful packaging. Better yet, some have made their packaging biodegradable. Some companies have reduced the amount of paper they use and increased their recycling efforts. Others have made their manufacturing processes more efficient, so they use less electricity. From installing compact fluorescent lightbulbs to turning down the thermostat, anything that saves electricity will help stop climate change.

WHAT CAN FARMERS DO?

Below: A bean leaf is infested with bugs at an organic farm in Maryland. Pesticides kill insects and protect crops, but also pollute waterways.

Soil is a carbon sink. It absorbs and stores more carbon dioxide than it produces. Carbon dioxide helps to make soil rich and full of nutrients. However, soil in much of North America has become depleted of nutrients.

Many farmers use herbicides to kill and prevent weeds. They use pesticides to kill insects. They use large amounts of cheap, synthetic fertilizer to help plants grow. Many farmers apply more fertilizer than plants can use, so it runs off into the waterways, killing fish. All these chemicals make the plants grow in the short term, but make the soil less fertile over the long term. Infertile soils don't hold carbon dioxide, which is released into the air.

Could farmers move to natural fertilizers and grow organic crops without the use of chemical fertilizers and pesticides? Many farmers already do that. Natural, sustainable farming creates rich soils and provides a natural carbon sink.

Above: Drew and Myra Goodman are cofounders of Earthbound Farm, one of the country's largest growers of organic produce. Many types of fruits and vegetables are grown on their California farm, as well as on other organic farms around the world. Even their packaging uses recycled plastic.

However, if all farmers suddenly stopped using chemical fertilizers and pesticides, would the insect population skyrocket? Would insects and invasive weeds destroy more crops? Would we suddenly have food shortages? These are important questions, and there are no easy answers. More research is needed to determine if stopping the use of chemical fertilizers and pesticides would cause further problems.

WHAT CAN LOCAL GOVERNMENTS DO?

Below: Some local governments offer their citizens rebates for purchasing energy-efficient appliances.

In the late 1990s and early 2000s, many city governments worried about climate change. They found themselves frustrated by the lack of action by national leaders. Some local governments decided to take action on their own. From California to Colorado to New York, local governments are trying to reform their cities the low-carbon way.

Above and Left: Owners of a Wisconsin inn stand next to their solar thermal system. They use solar power, a wind turbine, and a wood stove to meet the energy needs of their inn. Their electric meter spins backwards because of the power created by the wind turbine. Local governments often pay homeowners for the surplus energy generated by their equipment.

Many local governments have begun recycling programs. Others give rebates to households that buy new, energy-efficient appliances. Many counties offer free home energy audits. During an audit, a technician visits a home or business and suggests ways to increase energy efficiency.

Some counties now offer discounts to people who install solar power generators. Some counties put an extra tax on homes and businesses that use too much electricity. This tax motivates people to be more efficient.

Above: Solar panels are seen on the roofs of new homes in Apache Junction, Arizona.

Local governments also help by encouraging better buildings that use less electricity. Local governments can supplement the cost of solar shingles on homes. These shingles generate electricity by converting sunlight to electricity. Local governments can also encourage the building of wind and solar power plants.

Another way local governments can help is by making it possible to ride bikes and walk around the community instead of driving. Many cities have created miles of paths so that people can ride their bikes to work or to the store instead of driving.

Local governments have a huge opportunity to fight climate change. Local efforts may have as much, or even more, of an impact than national efforts. Any activity that reduces the burning of fossil fuels and takes low-mileage cars off the road is useful in keeping greenhouse gasses out of the atmosphere.

New York City has many bike lanes.

WHAT CAN CONSUMERS DO?

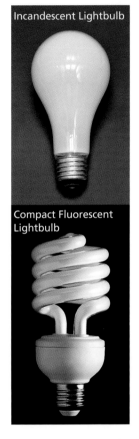

Incandescent Lightbulb

Compact Fluorescent Lightbulb

Above: Many people prefer to use energy-efficient compact fluorescent lightbulbs.

The things that people buy can have a big effect on the economy. For example, if everyone bought chocolate ice cream instead of vanilla, companies would quickly stop making vanilla ice cream. Consumers have a lot of power in determining what is produced. If people stop buying something, companies will stop making it.

Most of the electricity in North America comes from burning fossil fuels. Anything that uses less electricity, then, will cause a drop in fossil fuel burning. This, in turn, decreases the amount of greenhouse gasses in the atmosphere.

About 20 percent of our electricity is used to light our rooms, buildings, and streets. Compact fluorescent lightbulbs use only a fraction of the electricity used by incandescent lightbulbs. Compact fluorescent lightbulbs are more expensive, but they last much longer and are much more efficient. If everyone switched to compact fluorescent lights, it would save a big chunk of electricity.

Above: One 60-watt incandescent lightbulb uses as much electricity as four 13-watt fluorescent bulbs. Compact fluorescent lightbulbs also last up to 13 times longer, and each bulb generates nearly an equal amount of light.

Appliances such as refrigerators, furnaces, and dishwashers use a lot of electricity. Newer appliances use much less electricity than older versions. Replacing old appliances is another way to increase efficiency, use less electricity, and save money in the long run.

Some appliances and electronics are on all the time. Many televisions can be turned on by the remote control. This means that even when the television screen is off, the television is in stand-by mode. During stand-by mode, televisions continue to use a small amount of electricity. Most rechargers continue to draw electricity whenever they're plugged in. Some people estimate that about 10 percent of electricity is used by appliances in stand-by mode. Engineers sometimes call this "vampire load," because it sucks electricity all the time, without us even realizing it. People can save electricity by using power strips or by simply unplugging appliances and rechargers when not in use.

Below: Many electronic devices consume power even when they are not in use. It's estimated that about 10 percent of electricity is used by appliances recharging or on stand-by mode.

STAND BY
POWER

Above: An electric vehicle is plugged in and recharged at a London, England, "juice point." Many eager consumers are waiting for these new plug-in hybrids to become available around the world, which will greatly decrease gasoline usage.

Automobiles are a big source of carbon dioxide in the atmosphere. About a third of greenhouse gasses are emitted by cars and trucks. If consumers bought higher-mileage cars, that would make a huge dent in greenhouse gas emissions. Hybrid cars, which use both electricity and gasoline, can get 45 miles-per-gallon or more.

Many consumers are eager to buy a new class of cars called plug-in hybrids. These cars use electricity to run the car until the battery runs down. When that happens, a small gasoline engine recharges the battery. People can recharge their cars simply by plugging them into a wall outlet. These cars could greatly decrease the amount of gasoline needed.

WHAT CAN YOU DO?

O ne way to understand climate change is to study something called a carbon footprint. The average person in the United States uses a certain amount of electricity. The average person uses and discards a large amount of material, some of which may be recycled. The rest normally ends up in a landfill. The average person eats a variety of foods. Some of those foods are produced easily. Other foods require a lot of fertilizer or pesticides. Others, such as beef, require a lot of land for the animals to graze, a lot of water, and a lot of feed in order to raise the animal.

Facing Page and Below: Recycling is one way people can reduce their carbon footprints.

When these activities are added together, it is possible to calculate how much carbon dioxide the average person is responsible for creating. This is called a carbon footprint. In the United States, the average person's activities create about 20 tons (18 metric tons) of carbon each year. The average person in most other countries has a much smaller carbon footprint.

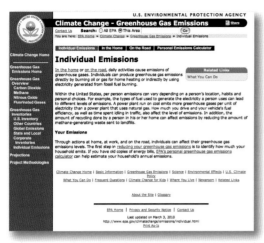

Above and Right: The U.S. Environmental Protection Agency (EPA) has a carbon calculator that allows people to calculate their individual and household emissions.

It is impossible to avoid creating a carbon footprint. However, our activities and choices can affect our carbon footprint's size. As we seek to reduce greenhouse gasses, reducing our carbon footprint is a good place to start. Many carbon footprint calculators exist online. Go to a search engine and type in "carbon footprint calculator" to estimate your own carbon footprint.

Part of reducing your carbon footprint is to recycle as much as possible. When we recycle a soda can, it means that less electricity will be needed to create a new can. When we reduce, reuse, and recycle, it goes a long way toward saving electricity, and therefore lowering greenhouse gasses.

Conserving electricity is another big part of reducing our carbon footprint. Using compact fluorescent lightbulbs and turning off lights and electronic devices when we are not in the room reduces our carbon footprint.

Encouraging parents to buy higher-mileage cars can help, too. Or better yet, ride a bicycle!

Above: The Hewlett-Packard recycling facility in Roseville, California, takes old computers and other electronic equipment and shreds them into pieces. The fragments are sorted into piles of steel, aluminum, plastic, and precious metals that are melted down and reused.

CLIMATE CHANGE CAN BE SOLVED

Facing Page: Renewable energy, such as wind and solar power, is helping to solve the problem of climate change.

Below: Individuals can do many things to lower their carbon footprint.

The solutions to climate change aren't difficult to understand. We must use less electricity, switch to renewable energy as quickly as possible, and reduce our carbon footprint. We must stop deforestation and use more sustainable farming methods.

However, those simple answers are very difficult to put into practice. They require that we change our activities, our ways of thinking, and our beliefs about the planet. We've always believed that the world was just too big for us to cause any problems. But that idea has been proven wrong.

It will also require much money to create new solar and wind energy initiatives. It will take money to reduce

our need for cheap but dirty fossil fuel plants. It will take money to help homeowners install solar collectors and wind power generators. It will take money to help car companies convert to higher-mileage cars.

It will be expensive to stop climate change. But the cost of doing nothing would be astronomical for us and for future generations.

GLOSSARY

BIODEGRADABLE

Waste material that can be broken down by living organisms such as bacteria.

CARBON DIOXIDE

Normally a gas, carbon dioxide is a chemical compound made of two oxygen atoms and one carbon atom. Its chemical symbol is CO_2. It is created by burning fossil fuels. It is the leading cause of the greenhouse effect and global warming.

CARBON FOOTPRINT

A measure of how much carbon is pumped into the atmosphere by a person's activities.

CARBON SINK

A natural area that absorbs and stores more carbon dioxide than it releases, such as a forest.

CLIMATE CHANGE

The climate of the earth, which consists of the weather all over the world for decades or centuries, and how it is changing.

FOSSIL FUEL

Fuels that are created from the remains of ancient plants and animals that were buried and then subjected to millions of years of heat, pressure, and bacteria. Oil and coal are the most common fossil fuels burned to create electricity. Natural gas is also a fossil fuel. Burning fossil fuels releases carbon dioxide into the atmosphere, contributing to global warming.

GREENHOUSE EFFECT

Just as heat is trapped in a greenhouse by glass, certain gasses in the atmosphere trap the sun's heat and warm the earth. The surface of the earth absorbs some solar radiation, and reflects some. The reflected rays either pass back into space, or are absorbed and reflected back by gasses in the earth's atmosphere. Carbon dioxide is a major greenhouse gas that is produced by burning fossil fuels. When too much solar radiation is absorbed, the earth warms up, which alters climates around the world.

GREENHOUSE GAS

Any gas that is good at absorbing and retaining the sun's heat. Carbon dioxide, which is released into the atmosphere by the burning of fossil fuels, is a greenhouse gas. Greenhouse gasses contribute to a gradual warming of the earth, which is called the greenhouse effect.

PHOTOVOLTAIC CELL

A device that generates electricity directly from the light of the sun.

PLUG-IN HYBRIDS

A type of car that runs on batteries. When the battery runs down, it is recharged by a small gasoline motor, or by plugging into an electrical outlet.

RENEWABLE ENERGY

Any kind of energy where the source won't get used up. Solar power, waterpower, and wind power are examples of renewable energy.

UNITED NATIONS

Formed in 1945, an organization of representatives from 192 nations with the mission of promoting peace, security, and economic development on a world-wide basis.

INDEX

Above: Carpooling is a way to reduce fossil fuel emissions.